Excel 2007

Tips and Tricks

First Published Mar 2013

Published by **everydayExcel Busines Lab Pte Ltd**

10 Anson Road #26-02A

International Plaza

Singapore 079903

Tel: +65 6226 1619

Fax: +65 3150 8248

Website: www.everydayexcel.com

Email: jason.khoo@everydayexcel.com

Table of Contents

1   Customize The Quick Access Toolbar (QAT)

This is also known as the QAT, in short. It's a very useful feature that has been overlooked after Excel 2003. Using the right icons can usually save you several steps. This is the default QAT, located above the Ribbon & consists of 3 icons (Save, Undo, Redo).

1.1   Show Below the Ribbon

One reason it's not being used as much is because of its location. So it's better to bring it below the ribbon, where you can <u>quickly</u> access it. To bring it down below the ribbon, click on the downward triangular dropdown. Then click on "Show Below the Ribbon".

After the selection, the QAT should be located here:

1.2   Default Icons from Dropdown

There are some default icons you can activate straight away from the dropdown.

Notice that those that currently exist in the QAT is being checked.

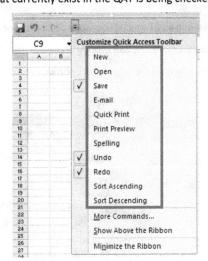

Here's how to create a new workbook using the Office Icon located on the top left hand corner of Excel:

First step, click on the "Windows" button.

Second step, click on "New".

Third Step, click on "Blank Workbook".

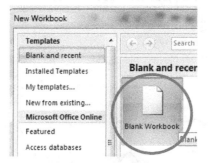

That is 3 steps in total. With the "New" icon, you just have to click it ONCE!

1.3   More Commands

Besides the default list, you can also consider putting in icons that you frequently use, so you can access it no matter which tab you are in. For eg, if you are always setting print area, you have to go to the "Page Layout" tab.

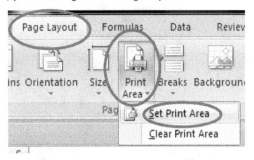

Once you are in other tabs, you have to go back to the "Page Layout" tab in order to set print area. Activate it in the QAT instead. Click on the dropdown on the QAT again & choose "More Commands".

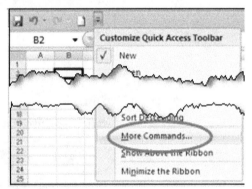

The default selection you see here is "Popular Commands". Scroll down the list shown below and look for "Set Print Area". If the list is too long, you can jump straight to the list starting with "s" by typing the letter "s on your keyboard.

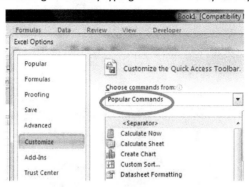

Scroll until you find "Freeze Panes" (Sorted alphabetically). Click on "Set Print Area" & then "Add"

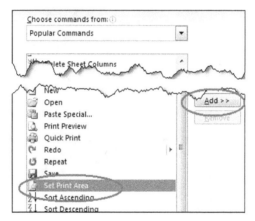

Once done, you should see it appearing on the right. You can then press OK below.

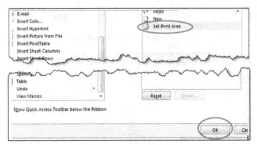

Now, even if you are in "Home" tab, you can set print area with one click:

2   Double Click On The Ribbon To Hide Them

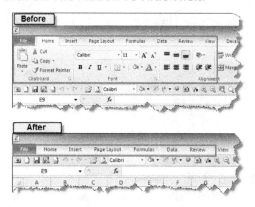

3   Quick Access To Frequently-Used Files

Thumbtacks are frequently used to place some important notes on the board.

Well, Excel has "thumbtacks" too. You can pin your frequently documents in the Recent Documents List, so that they stay there permanently like Favourites.

As seen in this list after clicking the Office button, the Recent Documents will keep updating with the latest file you opened listed at the top.

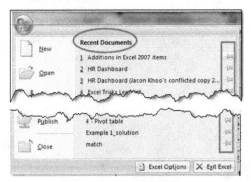

When you select the thumbtack on the right, it becomes green in colour, like a green pin used on the notice board. The files you have pinned will forever stay on the Recent Document list until you unpin them.

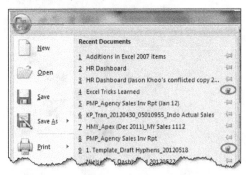

4   Tracking Real-Time Changes With Excel Camera

This function will help you track the changes in another range in your workbook as you change your inputs in another location.

Click on the QAT dropdown again & click on "More Commands"

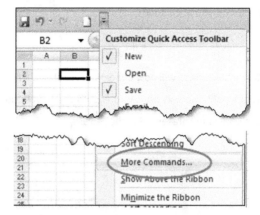

This time, click on "Popular Commands" to display dropdown list & choose "All Commands".

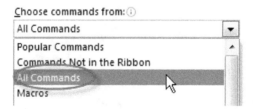

Click on any item in the list and then type the letter "c" on the keyboard. Then scroll down the list slowly until you find the command "Camera".

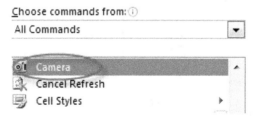

Add the camera into your QAT. Refer to the earlier topic on QAT to find out how to do it.

Once you have added in the camera, select C8:Y15 of the calendar.

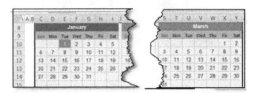

Click on the Camera icon you just added.

You will notice that a black cross will now appear in your sheet. Click inside the worksheet where the public holiday list is located. Add in a public holiday and the changes you made is instantly presented in the picture.

5   Jump Instantly To The End Of Your Database

To navigate quickly in a worksheet, you can use the [Ctrl] key and one of the 4

arrow keys. If there is nothing in the whole row and you press [Ctrl] + [→] arrow

key, it will bring you right to the end of the worksheet (Column XFD in Excel 2007).

If you have data, then [Ctrl] + [→] arrow key will bring you to the last cell that is

filled with data just before a blank cell.

It works the same when you try to use [←], [↑] or [↓] arrow keys.

6   Searching And Entering Formula With AutoComplete

Noticed how Google or YouTube recommends a list of keywords to search as you type into the search box? With the list, all you have to do is to use the arrow key to select the desired search phrase & press ENTER. Excel 2007 has something like this too.

In your selected cell, type the equal sign followed by the first character of your formula. A list of formulas matching the alphabet is immediately listed below. Select the formula using the UP & DOWN arrow keys. If the list is too long, type in another character. Once you have selected the formula from the list, hit the TAB key. The formula name is completed for you straight away. You can now enter the inputs for the formula using the mouse. When you added all your inputs, hit the ENTER key. Excel 2007 will close the bracket for you.

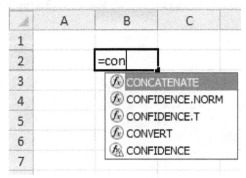

7   Create Attention Grabbing Comments

Click on the QAT dropdown button again & select "More Commands"

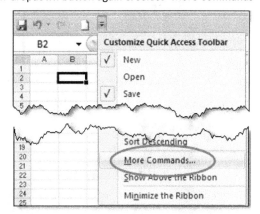

In the next dropdown shown below, choose "All Commands".

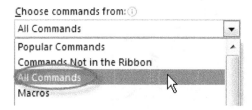

Look for the command "Change Shape" and select it.

Click on the Add button to add the "Change Shape" command to your Quick Access

Toolbar. Now, insert a comment into cell B5.

A normal comment box appears as shown below:

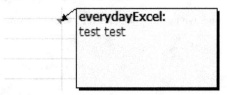

Select the comment box & click on the Change Shape icon. Choose a shape of your

choice. And your comments will be presented with a special shape.

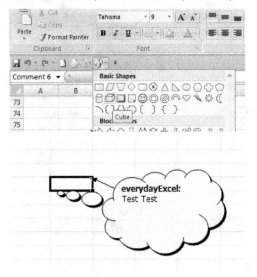

8   Using Customised Pictures In Charts

Create a column chart.

Find a picture that can effectively represent the data for your chart. Copy the picture.

Select the chart series.

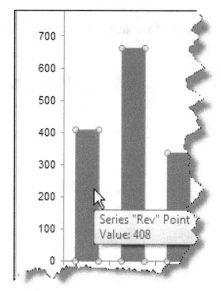

Click the Paste icon or use ⌨Ctrl + ⌨C .

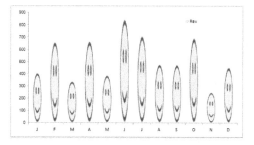

The columns are replaced with happy faces.

Right-click on the data series and select "Format Data Series".

Go to Fill -> Stack and scale with 100 units/picture or any other scale that is suitable for your chart. Click OK.

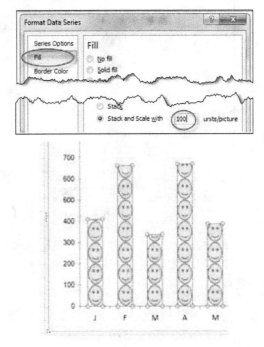

9   Add Pop-Up Comments Using Data Validation

Go to the "Data" tab -> Data Validation – Data Validation

Click on the "Input Message" tab, check the option of "Show input message when cell is selected" and input your message.

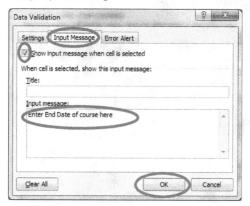

When you select the cell, the message will pop up as shown below.

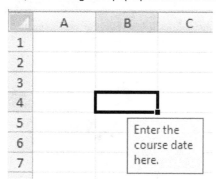

10   Highlight Data All At One Go With Find All

Press 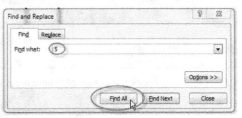 + to get to the Find window. Find "5" & press "Find All"

A list of results will appear.

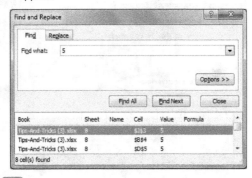

Press 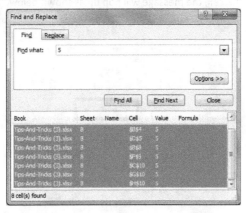 + to select all of them.

Close this Find window and you can now highlight all of them.

11   Finding Duplicates With Conditional Formatting

Select the range where you want to find the duplicates (for eg B2:B16 for this case).

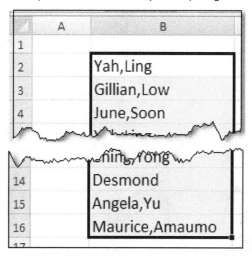

Go to the "Home" tab -> Conditional Formatting -> Highlight Cell Rules -> Duplicate

Values

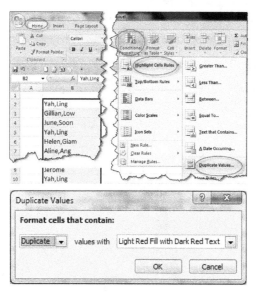

Click OK. All the names that appear more than once in the list are highlighted.

12   Filter Dates In Groups

When column data consist of only dates, there's a whole bunch of Date filters you could play with.

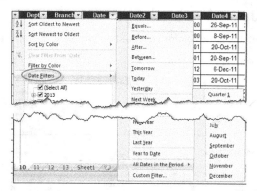

Alternatively, you can select Custom Filter and select the date range you require and click OK.

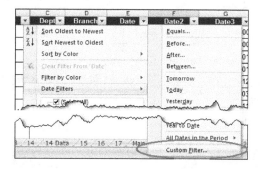

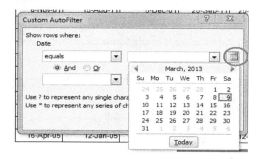

13   Removing Inconsistent Date Format Using TEXT to COLUMN

If you downloaded some data from the system and have a column of dates that are aligned partially to the left and right, don't use them. They are not usable. This is what you should do.

Select range containing the columns of date that you want to convert. Go to "Data" tab -> Text to Columns.

Choose Delimited and Next.

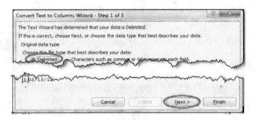

Do not choose any options here and click Next

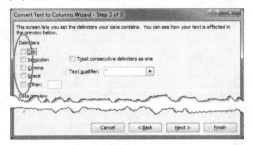

Check the Date option and select the date format that the current date is in. Then click Finish.

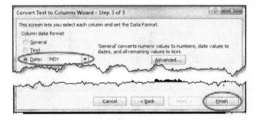

14   Converting Inconsistent Date Format Using Formulas

Using formulas, we can also convert them into actual dates recognised by Excel:

=DATE("20"&RIGHT(F2,2),LEFT(F2,2),MID(F2,4,2))

The DATE formula takes the last 2 digits of the date and joins it with 20 for the year

["20"&RIGHT(F2,2)], the left 2 numbers for the month [LEFT(F2,2)]and middle 2

digits for the day [MID(F2,4,2))].

Name	Dept	Branch	Date	Date1	Date2	
g	CPC RM	PRG	02.11.10	2/11/2010	11 02 10	11/2/2010

15   Highlight Dates Later Than Today Using Conditional Formatting

Select E2:M9 where the dates are:

Date	Date2	Date3	Date4	Date5
11-Feb-01	10-Aug-11	29-Sep-00	26-Sep-11	26-Mar-
16-Dec-10	21-Sep-12	27-Sep-00	8-Sep-11	27-Apr-
13-Mar-02	10-Aug-11	1-Jul-01	20-Oct-11	16-Apr
8-Nov-01	15-Aug-11	5-Dec-01	20-Sep-11	25-Oct-
17-Jan-03	22-Aug-11	21-Apr-12	6-Dec-11	30-Ju
	12-Apr-12	23-Apr-03	20-Oc	

Go to the "Home" tab -> Conditional Formatting -> Highlight Cell Rules -> Greater
Than...

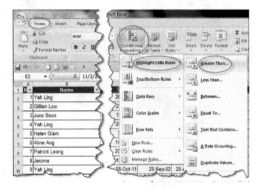

Fill in "1-jan-2012" for this

Dates later than 1-Jan-2012 are all highlighted.

16   Duplicating Pivot Table On The Fly

There is a quick way to churn out multiple pivot tables based on what you have in
the Report Filter of the Pivot Table. For example, if you want to have multiple pivot
tables with one worksheet per pivot table showing one country, do this.

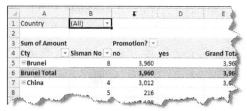

Click on any part of the Pivot Table and go to the "Options" tab (available only when
pivot table is selected).

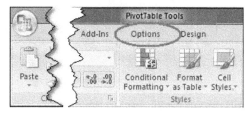

Go to the extreme left portion part of the ribbon where there is an Options
dropdown. Click on the dropdown and select "Show Report Filter Pages".

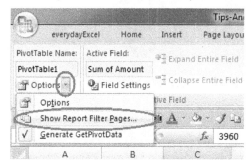

Select country and press OK.

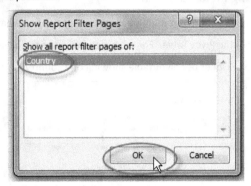

A pivot table is presented in one worksheet for every country found in the Pivot Table.

17   Removing Email Hyperlinks All At One Go

Type in "1" somewhere without the double quotes and click copy.

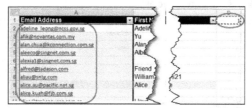

Select the column containing the hyperlinks. Go to the "Home" tab -> Paste -> Paste

Special.

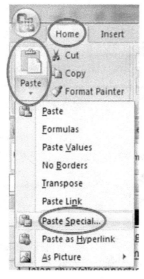

Select "Multiply" & click OK.

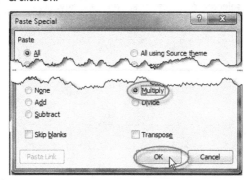

18   Removing Unwanted Objects All At One Go

Press the [F5] key & click on "Special".

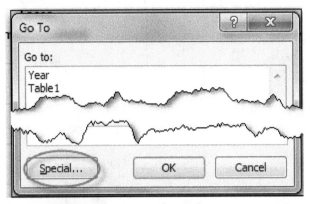

Select Objects & click OK.

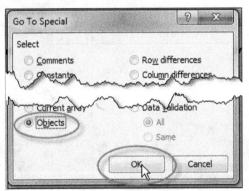

All objects will be selected & you can press the [Delete] key.

If you wish to delete objects in the specific range only, use the select object mode.

Activate the select object function.

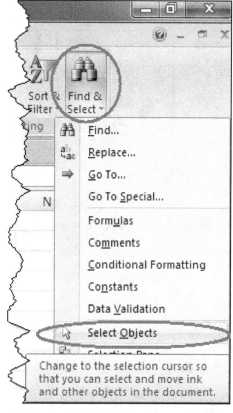

Using the cursor, select the area containing the objects you wish to delete.

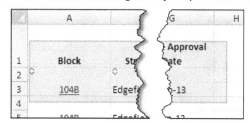

All the objects are now selected.

Press the Delete key to delete the selected objects

19   2 Rows Into One - Part I

Select the column or range containing the unwanted text.

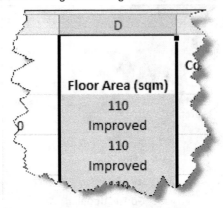

Press ⌨Ctrl + ⌨F to find. Find the text "Improved" without the double quotes and click on "Find All":

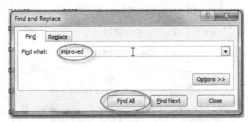

You should be able to see a list of results:

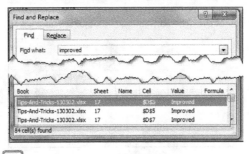

Press ⌨Ctrl + ⌨A to select them all. Once done. Close the Find window.

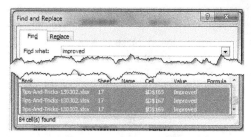

Go to the "Home" tab -> Delete -> Delete Sheet Rows

or simply use  +

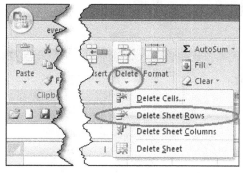

20 2 Rows Into One - Part II

The other method is to use Autofilter. Make sure all data is selected and go to the
"Data" tab -> Filter

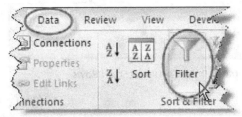

Go to the column you want to filter & click on the dropdown.

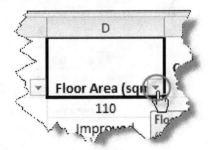

Checked on the item "Improved".

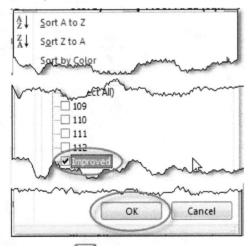

Select all the rows & press the ⬚F5 key. Choose "Special".

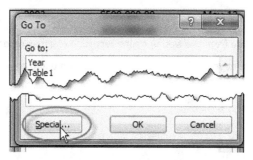

Choose "Visible cells only" and click OK.

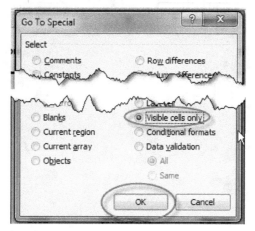

Delete the selected rows.

21   Convert Dates Using Formula

When you copy data from the web or online reports, Excel may recognise Feb-13 as 13-Feb of the current year. If this happens, use this formula to convert it to 1-Feb of that year (2013).

=DATE(DAY(I2)+2000,MONTH(I2),1)

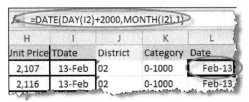

22   Creating A New Worksheet Using Mouse

On the extreme right where you see the sheet names, you can click on an icon to add new worksheets.

If you press the shift key, left click & hold on to your mouse on the sheet name, you should see a "+" sign appearing & a downward arrow on the left of the sheet name.

While you are still holding on the left click, shift it to the right of the sheet name to duplicate the worksheet.

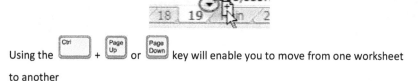

Using the [Ctrl] + [Page Up] or [Page Down] key will enable you to move from one worksheet to another

If you right-click on the arrow buttons on the left of the sheet names, you can see a list of your sheet names and you can select from the list the worksheet you want to go to.

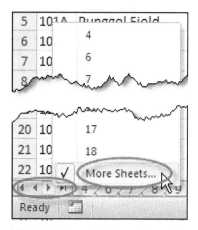

If all the worksheets cannot be displayed, click on "More Sheets" to select from the pop-up window.

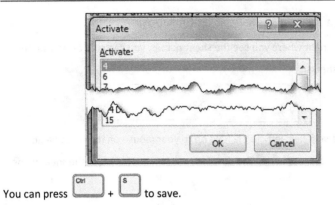

You can press ⌨Ctrl + ⌨S to save.

Using ⌨F12 can trigger the Save as key.

23   Filling In Pockets Of Blank Cells With Data

Click on the first cell you want to select (B2 for example). Use the scroll bar and scroll all the way down to the end.

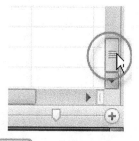

Press & hold on to the ⎡Shift⎤ key and left-click on the last cell you want to select (B319 for example). That should select all cells from B2:B319. Press the ⎡F5⎤ key & click on "Special".

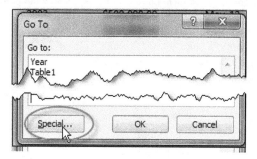

Select "Blanks" and click OK.

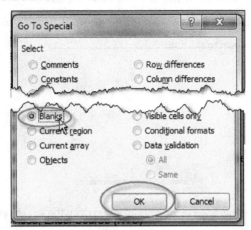

Only the blanks within B2:B319 will be selected now. Press the [=] key and click on the cell you want to use to fill in B6 (the 1ˢᵗ blank). That would be D6.

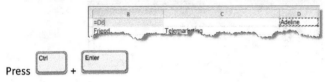

Press [Ctrl] + [Enter]

24   Presenting Your Numbers In Coloured Bars

Select a set of numbers in your report.

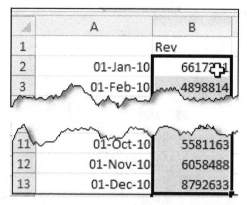

Go to "Home" tab -> Conditional Formatting -> Data Bars. Then select your desired
colour.

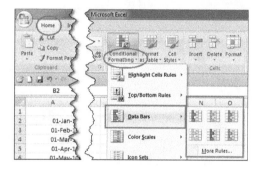

25   Using REPT Formula To Create In-Cell Scale

An alternative for Data Bars is using the formula REPT:

=REPT("|",B2/1000000)

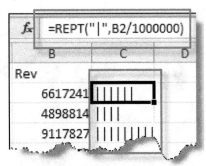

26   Removing Duplicates

Select the range containing the duplicates. Go to the "Data" tab -> Remove
Duplicates

Ensure that "My data has headers" is checked. Then check the relevant header(s)
used to determine a duplicate. Click OK when done.

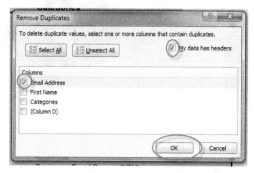

There will be a prompt to tell you how many records were removed and how many
unique records remain.

27   Adjusting The Formula Bar Using The Mouse

You can expand the formula bar if the formula is too long for 1 line. You should see a bi-direction arrow pointing up & down when you hover your mouse at the bottom edge of the formula bar.

Click & hold on to the left mouse button to expand the formula bar. You can do the reverse to revert.

28   Remove Unnecessary Spaces In The Description

To remove unnecessary spaces, you can use this formula:

=TRIM(A2)

To change the lettering from big capital letters to small capital letters, try this formula:

=LOWER(A2)

To change all the alphabets to big capital letters, use UPPER -> =UPPER(A2)

To change the first alphabet in each word to big capital letter, use PROPER ->

=PROPER(A2)

29   Clear All The Filters At One Go

Go to the "Data" tab -> Clear.

30 Tables, Auto-fill Formulas, Present Insert Cells, Auto Calculate The Total, Row Numbering

There are many great things you can do when you convert a data list into a table.

First, convert a data list into a Table by selecting the list and go to the "Insert" tab ->
Table

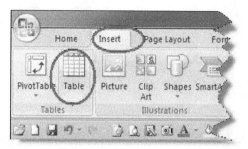

Enter a new formula into the first data row next to the table. The whole range is
automatically inserted with the new formula. If you change any formula withing the
table, it will be automatically updated to the rest of the rows.

My Table now has 266 rows including the header & excluding the Totals in row 267.

I have a formula **=ROW()-1** to give me the S/N number of the data.

N266	fx	=ROW()-1

	Country	Month	S/N
265	Thailand	25	264
266	Taiwan	28	265
267		2039	

If I press the **Tab** key on this row, it will create a new row for the Table. And any
cells with formulas will be copied down. As seen here, the Month & S/N column has
data in it because those are formulas. The Country column has to be manually filled
in though.

N267	fx	=ROW()-1

	Uountry	Month	S/N
265	Thailand	25	264
266	Taiwan	28	265
267		0	266
268		2039	

The Total row as seen here is also adjusted accordingly as the Table increases its data. Notice how the formula did not include a range like C2:C266 but a Name instead.

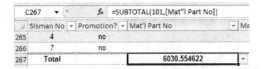

31   Auto-Refresh With Tables And Pivot Tables

If you create a Pivot Table using a Table as the source range, the table name will be captured in the source data box instead of a range. The pivot table will adjust its range automatically every time the table changes in size.

The only action left to do now is refresh the Pivot Table.

32   How To Create A Dropdown List - Data Validation, Limit Cell

Entry

Select the cells you want to add into the dropdown list, for example C1:C5. Go to

Data -> Data Validation.

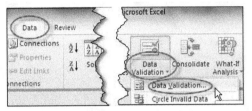

Select Allow: List -> Source:

=$A$2:$A$12

The source will be where you want to pick the list from.

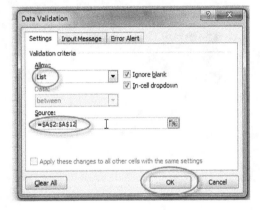